About Protecting Yourse Cyberwar

Protecting yourself in today's cyberwar is an event not like any other, and you need to prepare appropriately. You can't treat it like some other thing you might have experienced in the past. If you would like to succeed with safeguarding personal information, you ought to prepare every piece of yourself for the unique challenges which protecting yourself in today's cyberwar presents.

Protecting yourself in today's cyberwar is a progression that entails a great deal of groundwork. We will go over all the steps of the preparation process. This way you can really think of just how you would protect yourself in today's cyberwar. The first big thing to do is introspection. With this, you could be sure that protecting yourself in today's cyberwar is something you can honestly do.

Protecting yourself in today's cyberwar will not be the challenging part of training. Protecting yourself in today's cyberwar is a an extended process which entails approximately 5 days. It is smart to be as primed as possible prior to day one.

One of the smartest ways to decide whether you will be qualified to protect yourself in today's cyberwar is to evaluate the daily practices of individuals who already protect yourself in today's cyberwar regularly. You would not need to emulate their successes right away, since that might be cumbersome. However, you need to be primed to exert as much effort as they do. Imitate their practices, since they are specifically where you wish to be. Also, reflect on the below questions:

Do you have valuable information and assets that you want to protect?

Do you think your the best person to protect your information?

Can you afford to lose your identify and life savings?

These are certainly the sort of questions that a person who wants to protect yourself in today's cyberwar should reply yes to. By answering these particular questions affirmatively, that means that you have the personality type that ought to succeed in protecting yourself in today's cyberwar.

Below are some suggestions to help you to start:

-- Following up on every security email alert from companies you are affiliated with.

The key to prospering with protecting yourself in today's cyberwar is contingent upon following up on every security email alert from companies you are affiliated with., yet several people do not perceive just how critical that really is! Just by following up on every security email alert from companies you are affiliated with.. you would ensure that you're primed to protect yourself in today's cyberwar.

-- Getting a copy of your credit report.

Getting a copy of your credit report. helps you protect yourself in today's cyberwar. Understandably, that could be difficult to get in the routine of doing that. Begin getting a copy of your credit report. every day, and that ought to become habitual when you protect yourself in today's cyberwar.

-- Changing your passwords and make them more sophisticated after every nationwide data breach.

A big part of the discipline that is essential to protect yourself in today's cyberwar involves changing your passwords and make them more sophisticated after every nationwide data breach.. When you change your passwords and make them more sophisticated after every nationwide data breach., it prepares you to exist in the best physicality to realize the final objective of protecting yourself in today's cyberwar.

Protecting yourself in today's cyberwar entails tons of work spent over time. Consequently you can see, the best way to be primed for protecting yourself in today's cyberwar is to offer yourself the suggested amount of time for the preparations so you can flourish. Do that, and protecting yourself in today's cyberwar would be much easier.

Protecting Yourself In Today's Cyberwar - A Look Back

You should know that you are not the only person in the world that has the aspiration of protecting yourself in today's cyberwar. In actuality, there are tons of men and women everywhere that want to safeguard personal information. The bitter truth is that barely a few will really move forward and do it.

Don't reflect on endangering yourself to cyber attacks. Protecting yourself in today's cyberwar requires one to be protective and strong-willed. We understand that. Now we are able to investigate the stages recommended with protecting yourself in today's cyberwar so we can appreciate our future achievements.

You've already taken a huge step in becoming primed to protect yourself in today's cyberwar. Many people fail for good reason. They simply did not perceive what they were getting themselves into. Protecting yourself in today's cyberwar is that one thing in life that entails you to be completely steadfast and prepared. Just by looking further ahead and making sure you are protective and defensive, you are taking the first big step toward training.

Ask yourself one more time: Do you have valuable information and assets that you want to protect? Consider that question fully, because those who have successfully protect yourself in today's cyberwar possess one specific thing in common: they are definitely protective. You also ought to become protective if you expect to make your aspiration of protecting yourself in today's cyberwar a reality.

You have recently also figured out whether or not you are defensive after you were asked: Do you think your the best person to protect your information? Congratulations on making it this far, because that means you obviously have not surrendered. It is a huge difference between doing one thing and wanting to do something. This may come up quite a bit in safeguarding personal information.

Regardless of how far back you might care to look, you ought to find that those who are protecting yourself in today's cyberwar have one huge thing in common: they appreciated precisely what they were getting into. They all acknowledged precisely what it would be similar to, all that protecting yourself in today's cyberwar involved, coupled with all that was demanded of them to accomplish their goal. When you perceive precisely what it entails to protect yourself in today's cyberwar, there is nothing to stop you!

Being completely focused to protect yourself in today's cyberwar requires one to apply mentally, coupled with physically. The most effective technique to prepare all around is to have a strong mind and be mentally prepared.

Always remember that following up on every security email alert from companies you are affiliated with. is the most effective technique to assure your accomplishment. If you start feeling burned out, remember that by following up on every security email alert from companies you are affiliated with. in your preparations, you can be qualified to overcome this challenge. Let's move ahead to preparing to protect yourself in today's cyberwar.

Protecting Yourself In Today's Cyberwar In Everyday Life

Protecting yourself in today's cyberwar should be viewed as a culture. This is a critical part of the equation which you should incorporate in your lifestyle in numerous ways. So during the 5 days preparing to protect yourself in today's cyberwar, you could analyze how safeguarding personal information would change your life.

While you're getting your credit report and passwords available if they are not in your brain., thinking twice before you share personal information on social media sites. or monitoring credit and bank accounts cautiously., you may just be trying to attain general betterment. With focusing on the lifestyle, something will become crystal clear and you may see all that protecting yourself in today's cyberwar genuinely means to you. If you recognize the effects of protecting yourself in today's cyberwar, you may come to perceive that the effects are really what you are aiming to experience.

Additionally, someone needs to become defensive. This is not just a quality that is essential to protect yourself in today's cyberwar, but with other aspects of life.

The greatest thing about protecting yourself in today's cyberwar is the protective characteristic that is necessary to succeed which would make its way in other aspects of life. This causes you to feel like a more protective individual overall. Whenever you safeguard personal information, you are training your spirit for that which will follow. It is just one of the great things of protecting yourself in today's cyberwar.

Whenever you evaluate protecting yourself in today's cyberwar as a lifestyle instead of a goal, you may find it easier to adopt the habits that augments your success. The change in your routine has a bigger purpose beyond realizing a single goal.

Do you recall being asked:

Do you have valuable information and assets that you want to protect?

Do you think your the best person to protect your information?

Can you afford to lose your identify and life savings?

Along with looking at your life, these questions are also looking to assess your strengths and desires. So in the event you answered "yes" to those questions, there is an presumption of all that is of extreme importance to you.

Certainly no one ever stated that protecting yourself in today's cyberwar is simple, and definitely no one ever will. Protecting yourself in today's cyberwar would offer you tons of benefits coupled with skills to apply in life. Always remember, it would involve some time to get there. Protecting yourself in today's cyberwar can serve a critical role in your life by forcing you to have these good attributes.

If you are dedicated to completing whatever you set in motion, protecting yourself in today's cyberwar would become another marvelous thing which you do in your life. Best of wishes with beginning the progression towards a more rewarding lifestyle!

Why Protect Yourself In Today's Cyberwar

Protecting yourself in today's cyberwar has become an incredibly desired activity among people everywhere. There are countless intentions to protect yourself in today's cyberwar, which is the reason several people decide to endeavor it. Protecting yourself in today's cyberwar may be done to keep your life private, to keep your personal power, or to keep your headaches away. While the possible intentions for protecting yourself in today's cyberwar are endless, there would be a few that stand out as the most popular.

Keep Your Life Private

Protecting yourself in today's cyberwar to keep your life private is a great reason to safeguard personal information. Whenever you have a specific reason to protect yourself in today's cyberwar, that makes the aspiration more meaningful. Then when you finally secure yourself from today's cyberwar, it should feel more fulfilling.

Keep Your Personal Power

A common reason that several people choose to protect yourself in today's cyberwar is to keep your personal power. This is a great reason to protect yourself in today's cyberwar as well.

Keep Your Headaches Away

A different reason which people choose to protect yourself in today's cyberwar is to keep your headaches away. Safeguarding personal information is a tough undertaking. When you protect yourself in today's cyberwar successfully, you may also develop a unique relationship with others who have also protect yourself in today's cyberwar.

Overall, protecting yourself in today's cyberwar would bring a large feeling of accomplishment to your life, and with good reason. Priming for this is an exciting experience, which is the one reason that many people choose to safeguard personal information. Also, protecting yourself in today's cyberwar may also offer you a clear perspective on existence. And after you protect yourself in today's cyberwar, you should recognize that you can achieve just about anything in this world. That is, if you clear your mind and do it. The intentions to protect yourself in today's cyberwar are definitely different from one individual to the next. So ultimately, you need to endeavor it for your own individual reasons.

Things To Do Before Protecting Yourself In Today's Cyberwar

A guide full of things to achieve before protecting yourself in today's cyberwar would rapidly fill up lots of full-length books. Protecting yourself in today's cyberwar is difficult. It is obviously reflected in the large amount of coaching material existent to anyone aiming to safeguard personal information. Despite this fact, there are some key ways which a guard could make to their regimented process. It also, doesn't matter how seasoned that guard is; you could make it work. The most critical factor to keep in your thoughts is that you'd have to train, both physically and mentally.

Getting your credit report and passwords available if they are not in your brain. is the key with a routine. You may never be qualified to protect yourself in today's cyberwar if you just work on training a little bit once in a blue moon. Complete a regimented process and stick with it. It is all right to take some time off every now and then, but you need to be fairly steadfast with training each day. Getting your credit report and passwords available if they are not in your brain. everyday would help you in a multitude of ways. You would even start to think differently.

You will be better primed for any challenge because you will be stronger. You will also feel better about yourself overall. Remember that you are a protective individual, and you need to make the necessary modifications to reflect that. Get in the regiment of getting your credit report and passwords available if they are not in your brain. so you are typically feeling confident and in control. and feeling ready.

Equally critical as getting your credit report and passwords available if they are not in your brain. is thinking twice before you share personal information on social media sites.. If you observe people who have productively protect yourself in today's cyberwar, you would see that they typically think twice before you share personal information on social media sites.. It is because they perceive the necessity of this practice. Thinking twice before you share personal information on social media sites. results in protecting your information. It is well known that thinking twice before you share personal information on social media sites. also would control your identity. Stop sending unsolicited information to people you do not know. It would dispatching unsolicited information should be stopped so you will not get unsolicited viruses in return.

Crowds of individuals may agree that they would be relieving stress, merely by thinking twice before you share personal information on social media sites.. That would get your brain on organizing your daily duties to protect yourself in today's cyberwar. While safeguarding personal information, that should help you to be mindful of the reason you are doing it all in the first place. You will also remember which guidelines and methods have served you before.

Another great benefit that a guard has is while they monitor credit and bank accounts cautiously.. They is preventing identify theft. Being ready to protect yourself in today's cyberwar rapidly is important. But that would be futile if you are incapable of protecting yourself in today's cyberwar for a long time. Monitoring credit and bank accounts cautiously. has a multitude of constructive effects which go beyond safeguarding personal information. Monitoring credit and bank accounts cautiously. results in preventing identify theft coupled with knowing your credit and bank account activity..

There are a few additional concerns to be mindful of while you are monitoring credit and bank accounts cautiously.. Report any and all unusual activity. It would directly yield a better result to update all activity. In addition, monitoring credit and bank accounts cautiously. would help you to monitor your credit score. And by developing a really optimistic point-of-view, it will help you with any discouraging weeks you may experience. Think about whatever you should try to improve your decisions, and proceed from there. An optimistic point-of-view would make all the difference while you are protecting yourself in today's cyberwar.

Definitive Mistakes Made While You Protect Yourself In Today's Cyberwar

Of course, there are a few steps that you'll not want to endeavor when safeguarding personal information. While a new guard may make a few slips, there are two in particular that you'd want to prevent at all costs.

Do not forget to shred personal information. It would cause you to fall back in all of your efforts. Why would a person put forth all that effort just to reverse whatever they have done? This is what takes place when you forget to shred personal information.

There is an action that would help you prevent certain blunders from happening. If you have been safeguarding personal information for a while, take a little time off to break up the preparations involved.

Also, do not give your social security number out like it's halloween candy. It is the other critical blunder that any guard could avoid. While there are lots of ways to safeguard personal information, practicing these suggestions would yield a positive ending no matter what. Assuming you are smart with your duties and follow through the preparation period, then you should be qualified to secure yourself from today's cyberwar.

Rules to Consider While Protecting Yourself In Today's Cyberwar

As we've recently analyzed, protecting yourself in today's cyberwar requires quite a bit out of a person. They must be protective, defensive, as well as securing. Many individuals may develop these particular traits, but realistically the fact is that preparing for an experience as impacting as protecting yourself in today's cyberwar may really strip these great traits away from you. Below are a few rules you could heed that'll help your inner self nurture these particular traits.

Preparing yourself for the tough task of protecting yourself in today's cyberwar is certainly time-consuming, and you'll presumably be investing close to 5 days to prepare. This ought to offer you sufficient time to ingrain these particular rules in your routine.

Just Remember to know exactly where your passwords and and credit report are. This will equipped to take on the cyber attack immediately. It is one of the numerous positive results that this habit will yield. In addition, you will feel confident and in control., especially when the moment comes to actually protect yourself in today's cyberwar.

Also Stop sending unsolicited information to people you do not know. This is certainly an ideal rule to incorporate while you are thinking twice before you share personal information on social media sites.. This would dispatching unsolicited information should be stopped so you will not get unsolicited viruses in return. If you see yourself as defensive, then it may be straightforward for you to heed these rules in your lifestyle.

Let us remember this goal of monitoring credit and bank accounts cautiously.. It may take yet another degree of focus during the preparation stage, but it will be worth it. During the time you are succeeding toward knowing your credit and bank account activity. and monitoring your credit score, you should Report any and all unusual activity. Just by making certain that you maintain this mindset, you might update all activity.

Protecting yourself in today's cyberwar isn't like endangering yourself to cyber attacks. While anybody can attempt to safeguard personal information, it requires one who's securing and protective to really realize this objective of protecting yourself in today's cyberwar.

When you are completely dedicated, you can achieve anything! Think back to the below questions:

Do you have valuable information and assets that you want to protect?

Do you think your the best person to protect your information?

Can you afford to lose your identify and life savings?

You proved you are protective, defensive, and securing by saying "yes" to all of these questions. Whenever you protect yourself in today's cyberwar, these attributes ought to help you. If you apply these vital practices, and you get your credit report and passwords available if they are not in your brain., think twice before you share personal information on social media sites., and monitor credit and bank accounts cautiously., then you'll become a accomplishment in no time!

What You Need to Know Before Protecting Yourself In Today's Cyberwar

We discussed a couple of the assorted practices that a person who wants to protect yourself in today's cyberwar could reflect on carrying out. Since you have learned the choices of one wanting to protect yourself in today's cyberwar, the probability is that some choices are spliced into your daily decisions already. You could explore how you can bolster those characteristics into a substantial part of your routine. This would make preparing to protect yourself in today's cyberwar an easy evolution.

After all, preparing to realize the final objective would require you to carry out a couple adjustments in your decisions. Your openness to growing would be the determining factor in how rapidly you accomplish your ambitions.

Are you primed to get a copy of your credit report.? Are you primed to change your passwords and make them more sophisticated after every nationwide data breach. and follow up on every security email alert from companies you are affiliated with.? These are just a few practices to equip you toward the progression of protecting yourself in today's cyberwar. If that looks distressing, do not agonize. We have a couple suggestions pertaining to meeting your ambitions.

Don't skip through the introductory steps.

Occasionally it looks as if the introductory steps may be neglected. Feasibly you may feel you may prevail without carrying out steps like getting a copy of your credit report.. There may presumably come a point after starting the preparation of protecting yourself in today's cyberwar when you may face a task similar to getting your credit report and passwords available if they are not in your brain.. Assuming you executed the introductory steps noted, you may face a much easier time meeting your ambitions.

Investing a pre-determined timeframe merely to narrow in on the little steps is best. It may cause the following steps of your progression to be smoother. Lastly, you would be fully primed to protect yourself in today's cyberwar after the preparation.

Do not call it quits if you fail preparing.

However meaningful your effort may be, expect problems. Instead of striving for perfection, try following the introductory steps for the majority of the time. This may offer you a safeguard to botch up the steps periodically. If you anticipate stumbling from perfection periodically, that would prevent you from giving up while you sway from the steps of protecting yourself in today's cyberwar.

Identify theft at an all time high, credit card and bank card numbers are primary targets. Hack proof radio frequency identification (RFID) wallets and purses help you from ID theft.

It might sound like an indisputable thing to achieve while you are priming to protect yourself in today's cyberwar. However it is startling how some people fail getting appropriate supplies beforehand. This is an easy tip to try. Do not make the most critical mistake of darting over these imperative preparations.

Make yourself a list of all your potential items that are high risk of identify theft.

Whether you're attempting to accomplish a physical aspiration or a critical part of the equation which entails more mental stamina, your brain leads whatever you do. That is the reason, it is critical to prepare your mind toward the work at hand. If the mind is tailored with the work at hand, that makes carrying out the work quicker. What we do starts with a hope. Plant constructive ideas in your brain, and the progression to protect yourself in today's cyberwar should be ultimately underway.

If you reflect on calling it quits, do not.

It is common to become discouraged while things become difficult. If protecting yourself in today's cyberwar was painless, everyone will be doing it. The fact is that protecting yourself in today's cyberwar entails a little effort and intentional action. The advantages would be really rewarding. Even though you might want to call it quits while things are difficult, do not. Do not call it quits since you can do this!

Ignore the perceptions you have regarding protecting yourself in today's cyberwar.

With TV, the Internet and social media so rampant in our routine, it is likely to have preconceived ideas about protecting yourself in today's cyberwar. Most of the perceptions regarding protecting yourself in today's cyberwar are not exactly accurate. Assume difficult effort and dedication to attain the ambitions of protecting yourself in today's cyberwar. However you evaluate it, a protective and defensive self-starter would succeed at protecting yourself in today's cyberwar. If you are unable to identify yourself as defensive and protective today, do not agonize. These attributes are fostered and you need to develop your mind to become protective and defensive.

Get in the habit of destroying any and all information that has your name, social security number, address or any other personal information before you put it in the trash. A small paper shredder may be the answer for you.

While protecting yourself in today's cyberwar starts with a progression with your mind, there is the physical aspect which is just as essential. While the mind is in a suitable place, you really have to also do the physical steps. These suggestions are so critical because that centers upon the physical aspect of protecting yourself in today's cyberwar.

These are very definite practices which would prepare you for the experience. You need to plan to put in about 5 days to safeguard personal information. Before this 5 days starts, you need to be practicing these specific suggestions. A practice entails a moment to put into action. It starts with an undertaking in the mind. Maintain a notebook to track the progress and that would help you to remain on path.

If you fall off path, get right back on. Protecting yourself in today's cyberwar is a progression and periodically you may fall off path. The critical thing is that you get right back on! Also, make sure that you're basking in your experience. Anybody who yearns to protect yourself in today's cyberwar wants to receive some mental satisfaction from it. Additionally feed off the recognition you receive along the way while you finally secure yourself from today's cyberwar!

The Easiest Way To Protect Yourself In Today's Cyberwar

While there are plenty of guides available strictly about protecting yourself in today's cyberwar, there's one thing they all convey: the preparation phase is definitely critical. A decent amount of time to safeguard personal information is approximately 5 days. Priming for so long grants you the essential stamina to protect yourself in today's cyberwar.

You're now ultimately ready to jump into the work at hand. But, first we'll examine a few constructive habits. This way you are as primed as possible the moment you protect yourself in today's cyberwar. The next steps that you could do to get ready to protect yourself in today's cyberwar are: get a copy of your credit report., change your passwords and make them more sophisticated after every nationwide data breach. and follow up on every security email alert from companies you are affiliated with.. Together these tips produce a solid core for your preparations.

Preparing for a minimum of 5 days before you protect yourself in today's cyberwar is definitely critical, and can't be emphasized enough. It allows you to completely prepare. Additionally, it grants you these three beneficial practices essential for protecting yourself in today's cyberwar. You should find that getting your credit report and passwords available if they are not in your brain., thinking twice before you share personal information on social media sites., and monitoring credit and bank accounts cautiously. will assure that you exert your greatest effort possible.

If you ignore these particular instructions, you would forego feeling confident and in control., feeling ready, and relaxing the mind. These results all stem from the preparation phase.

With the appropriate groundwork and process, you would also be preventing identify theft, knowing your credit and bank account activity. coupled with monitoring your credit score. Every one of those are definitely critical to achieve protecting yourself in today's cyberwar. The greatest part of it is, if you put forth a bit of effort into preparing, then it might ultimately be quite simple for you. So keep from darting over the introductory steps. And conclusively, be sure that you are completely ready.

Many, people erroneously feel that it would be difficult, or even impossible to become a accomplishment. In actuality, it just requires one who is protective, defensive and securing to physically go through the preparatory stages. If you completely commit to not taking short-cuts in the preparation period and finish all of the steps necessary, then you are perfectly positioned to protect yourself in today's cyberwar.

In closing, the most simple technique to protecting yourself in today's cyberwar is to incorporate all of the steps laid out here. Consequentially, cutting corners is not worth the effort and ought to be avoided when safeguarding personal information. You need to devote your time on the preliminary process of the procedure since it should make you more successful. The fact is 5 days is really not a huge amount of time to prepare for such a challenging event as protecting yourself in today's cyberwar. So, make the pledge, put forth the demanded amount of time, and you can be protecting yourself in today's cyberwar in no time!

Protecting Yourself In Today's Cyberwar For Free

You may feel that it takes a good deal of cash to protect yourself in today's cyberwar, but in fact you can safeguard personal information for free. The obvious thing you could do when you start to safeguard personal information is to eliminate the existing concerns you might have regarding what it is like.

There are a few rudimentary suggestions which would help you stabilize your target of protecting yourself in today's cyberwar with your pocketbook. Start with a free copy of your credit report each year. You can get a free copy at www.annualcreditreport.com. You may want to look into their identity protection program or look into their real-time alerts. If you intentionally concentrate your energy on luxuries that do not need a lot of money, then you permit yourself to narrow in on the things you ought to be carrying out. Remember, getting your credit report and passwords available if they are not in your brain., thinking twice before you share personal information on social media sites. coupled with monitoring credit and bank accounts cautiously. are steps that are of utmost importance and would not require tons of money.

There are other steps you may also do, in order to invest minimal money. Attempt to keep all your personal information private. Go the extra mile and give unsolicited callers zero information. Sometimes it's best to hang up the phone before they can even verify your name. You would not need to put forth a good deal of money to safeguard personal information. Whenever you intentionally put your emotions aside regarding money, then you could find several inexpensive luxuries which are most likely adequate compared to the more cost prohibitive ones. That is an easy option when your objectives are the focal point.

During the time you are monitoring credit and bank accounts cautiously., achieve it with a mindset to save cash. No more 1, 2, 3, A, B, C, passwords! Using names and birth dates can be cracked easy. Create passwords that only you know and put them in your lock box. During the time you are protecting yourself in today's cyberwar you do not need to squander cash on overly expensive items when there are inexpensive options which work equally as good. Many people were protecting yourself in today's cyberwar before several of the more expensive items were created. If they did not require it, then you should not either.

The obvious thing that you could do is to always be focused on your goal. Also, thinking twice before you share personal information on social media sites., monitoring credit and bank accounts cautiously. and getting your credit report and passwords available if they are not in your brain. are a few of the best steps that you could be focused upon. Just by typically looking at decisions through the eyes of your goal, you should recognize which expenses are luxuries that you do not genuinely need.

Getting your credit report and passwords available if they are not in your brain. doesn't need a lot of money. The goal is to feel confident and in control., and that could be attained with minimal spending since it doesn't have to be cost prohibitive. In actuality, it usually takes more to not think twice before you share personal information on social media sites.. The reason you need to narrow in on thinking twice before you share personal information on social media sites. is so you can protect your information. Again, that doesn't need a lot of spending to attain.

Lastly, focus a bit of effort on thinking twice before you share personal information on social media sites., coupled with how you could monitor credit and bank accounts cautiously. correctly. Do not permit yourself to become swamped by items which involve excessive spending. Remember, there are adequate options available to monitor credit and bank accounts cautiously. that are low in cost.

The final summation is, if you would be steadfast on your objectives, then you could avert pointless spending to attain your goal of protecting yourself in today's cyberwar. There are always options available that are low in cost. Understanding how your emotions sway your spending ought to allow you to manage costs while you are working towards protecting yourself in today's cyberwar.

Protecting Yourself In Today's Cyberwar - Step by Step

At this point, it's obvious which sort of individual is required to actually protect yourself in today's cyberwar. We have also learned more of all the attributes that one definitely needs in order to safeguard personal information. So now, we can now get on with the things we are set to do.

Without a doubt, the preliminary step is confirming that you are definitely getting your credit report and passwords available if they are not in your brain. since it can establish your readiness to protect yourself in today's cyberwar. You could think of getting your credit report and passwords available if they are not in your brain. as this: no individual can possibly safeguard personal information without too getting your credit report and passwords available if they are not in your brain.. It is completely impossible - that is just how imperative this step is.

Getting your credit report and passwords available if they are not in your brain. has lots of great benefits. For example, it typically results with you feeling confident and in control.. Lacking that, it would become next to impossible to protect yourself in today's cyberwar. One other great benefit with getting your credit report and passwords available if they are not in your brain. is it will have you feeling ready when relaxing the mind.

You would also have to continue thinking twice before you share personal information on social media sites. all through your preparations, and also while you protect yourself in today's cyberwar. To safeguard personal information is incredibly difficult, but fortunately thinking twice before you share personal information on social media sites. ought to help. Plus, getting your credit report and passwords available if they are not in your brain. would help you start protecting your information, which is obviously important. Protecting your information ought to help you while you safeguard personal information now and in the future.

Thinking twice before you share personal information on social media sites. also extends more benefits in other ways outside of protecting yourself in today's cyberwar. It might help you control your identity and relieve stress. Also controlling your identity is equally critical whether you are protecting yourself in today's cyberwar or not. So, you should try executing any method that gets you controlling your identity.

After investing time toward getting your credit report and passwords available if they are not in your brain. and thinking twice before you share personal information on social media sites., you may feel you are primed to protect yourself in today's cyberwar. Regardless of your perceptions, be sure to analyze whether or not you really are or if it's just your mind causing you to feel you are. Many people who would like to protect yourself in today's cyberwar invest up to 5 days training.

One other factor that is necessary to help you become successful with protecting yourself in today's cyberwar is monitoring credit and bank accounts cautiously.. You would not need to narrow in on monitoring credit and bank accounts cautiously. until the latter half of the preparations, however certainly do not move past it altogether. Monitoring credit and bank accounts cautiously. could lead you to prevent identify theft, and would be beneficial towards the preparations. It also pushes you to know your credit and bank account activity. and monitor your credit score, which then pushes you to protect yourself in today's cyberwar.

Lastly, you'll be primed to protect yourself in today's cyberwar by getting your credit report and passwords available if they are not in your brain., thinking twice before you share personal information on social media sites. and monitoring credit and bank accounts cautiously.. It typically requires 5 days of the preparation period to be completely ready. But, that amount of time ought to go by really rapidly. If you designate a fixed date to initialize your preparation period and mark 5 days later, then it will allow your brain to already see that timeframe as the preparatory process. At that point, you'll be able to narrow in on getting your credit report and passwords available if they are not in your brain., coupled with thinking twice before you share personal information on social media sites.. Thereafter, you'll find that your entire mind is completely ready to protect yourself in today's cyberwar!

Strategies To Protecting Yourself In Today's Cyberwar

Protecting yourself in today's cyberwar entails a lot from a person. Unfortunately, everyone doesn't really possess all that it takes. There are definitely some specific strategies that work better than others to assure that you are always training for your ambitions the best way. Recognizing this ought to allow you to finally protect yourself in today's cyberwar.

For example, a individual who tends to be careless or uncertain may not be that successful when protecting yourself in today's cyberwar. They would have the attributes of one who answered no to the following question:

Do you have valuable information and assets that you want to protect?

If you wish to protect yourself in today's cyberwar, some attributes are needed. Being protective is an actual requirement. If you wish to accomplish your aspiration of protecting yourself in today's cyberwar and ultimately feel like a accomplishment, then you will have to become defensive.

Anybody can shout that they wish to protect yourself in today's cyberwar. However, protecting yourself in today's cyberwar is a large step above endangering yourself to cyber attacks. One doesn't involve a good deal of preparation, whereas preparation is certainly critical to the overall outcome with the other.

Safeguarding personal information requires getting a copy of your credit report.. This may not seem like a huge issue, when compared to protecting yourself in today's cyberwar, but realistically getting a copy of your credit report. is very critical while you protect yourself in today's cyberwar.

Changing your passwords and make them more sophisticated after every nationwide data breach. is also essential when it comes to planning to protect yourself in today's cyberwar. It makes perfect sense just how critical changing your passwords and make them more sophisticated after every nationwide data breach. is to safeguard personal information.

Following up on every security email alert from companies you are affiliated with. may too not seem like a huge thing, however it definitely is. When protecting yourself in today's cyberwar, you will need the preparations which you spent time on.

Safeguarding personal information and afterwards protecting yourself in today's cyberwar to become a accomplishment, would help you now and after your intentional actions. You should find feeling confident and in control., protecting your information, and preventing identify theft all stem from you protecting yourself in today's cyberwar. Safeguarding personal information is desired by lots of people because they perceive the benefits that protecting yourself in today's cyberwar brings.

When you implement the various tactics in order to protect

yourself in today's cyberwar, you'll find your present traits greatly improved. Any protective individual ought to become more protective. Any defensive individual ought to be more defensive. And any securing individual ought to become more securing. This is the reason there's definitely no better moment to start than now!

Tips To Protect Yourself In Today's Cyberwar Better

Protecting yourself in today's cyberwar would be a life-changing responsibility, but fortunately there are methods to make your life a bit more manageable while you are safeguarding personal information. Below are a few ways for protecting yourself in today's cyberwar which would help you.

- Already examined in the preparation period of protecting yourself in today's cyberwar was the necessity of getting your credit report and passwords available if they are not in your brain.. It is critical that when you get your credit report and passwords available if they are not in your brain., you Remember to know exactly where your passwords and and credit report are. This would help equipped to take on the cyber attack immediately. This is critical not just when preparing for protecting yourself in today's cyberwar, but in different aspects as well.

- You should know that thinking twice before you share personal information on social media sites. is essential as well. It may become difficult to do on your own. So a great technique to dispatching unsolicited information should be stopped so you will not get unsolicited viruses in return is to Stop sending unsolicited information to people you do not know. This ought to offer you additional incentive to think twice before you share personal information on social media sites. as you prepare to protect yourself in today's cyberwar.

- Additionally, know that protecting yourself in today's cyberwar definitely needs you to constantly monitor credit and bank accounts cautiously.. In order to update all activity, it makes sense to Report any and all unusual activity.

During the time you incorporate these simple suggestions in your preparation with protecting yourself in today's cyberwar, you will find that you would be gaining numerous benefits. Below are a few benefits which you may see after you follow through your commitments to protect yourself in today's cyberwar:

- During the time you get your credit report and passwords available if they are not in your brain., you may start feeling confident and in control..

- Getting your credit report and passwords available if they are not in your brain. would also help you feel ready.

- Thinking twice before you share personal information on social media sites. would result in protecting your information.

- In addition, thinking twice before you share personal information on social media sites. helps with controlling your identity.

- As you strive to monitor credit and bank accounts cautiously., you should find that you are knowing your credit and bank account activity..

- Monitoring credit and bank accounts cautiously. also will know your credit and bank account activity..

Safeguarding personal information grants a lot of direct benefits, a few of which we have successfully discussed. , relieving stress, and relaxing the mind all happen when you are getting your credit report and passwords available if they are not in your brain., thinking twice before you share personal information on social media sites., and monitoring credit and bank accounts cautiously.. Safeguarding personal information entails carrying out all of these particular steps and reveling in the benefits that follow. In addition, these are a few additional tips:

- Start with a free copy of your credit report each year. You can get a free copy at www.annualcreditreport.com. You may want to look into their identity protection program or look into their real-time alerts.

- Attempt to keep all your personal information private. Go the extra mile and give unsolicited callers zero information. Sometimes it's best to hang up the phone before they can even verify your name.

- No more 1, 2, 3, A, B, C, passwords! Using names and birth dates can be cracked easy. Create passwords that only you know and put them in your lock box.

Protecting yourself in today's cyberwar takes a good deal of work. Luckily, if you use all of the help offered here while you safeguard personal information, then you ought to be more than qualified by the end of the 5 days to protect yourself in today's cyberwar.

Though remember, these suggestions are merely a starting point. When you are completely done looking at this information, you should perceive all that is demanded to protect yourself in today's cyberwar. Apply these reflections to become better, and you would be able in no time.

The Best System For Protecting Yourself In Today's Cyberwar

There are tons of strategies existent to individuals thinking about protecting yourself in today's cyberwar, and they all proclaim to be the most simple. In fact, a couple of these particular strategies, which you may find online, assure better benefits. However, the accomplishment of protecting yourself in today's cyberwar depends upon each individual coupled with their point-of-view towards preparing. A great guard would be a great guard regardless what the circumstances. Equally, a bad guard would continue to become worse whether they are protecting yourself in today's cyberwar as a beginner, or are more seasoned in their craft. Protecting yourself in today's cyberwar is a mental activity equally as much as it is a physical one.

Over the 5 days of preparing leading up to this big day, you may become fairly busy preparing in advance. Not only does safeguarding personal information physically challenge you, but it also stimulates your brain. In regards to preparing the general plan, multi-faceted legwork is certainly critical. There are tons of tools handy to help determine the particulars of protecting yourself in today's cyberwar. Though, your individual judgment will be better compared to any tool. After all, you perceive your body and characteristic nature like no one else. Utilize that know-how to calculate your target and do not ignore your intuition since it's not likely to misguide you.

We figured that the normal timeframe one prepares to protect yourself in today's cyberwar is 5 days. So, you need to be generous when preparing your time. Remember, you perceive your body better than anyone. If you require more time, do not stress yourself trying to attain your aspiration in specifically 5 days. Do the calculations and figure out the time you'd require. Lastly, update your objectives accordingly.

During the time you prepare to protect yourself in today's cyberwar, you might find additional individuals who are trying to accomplish the same objective. Remember, they are most likely working with a separate timeframe than you. So, do not become caught up wrestling with their schedule or methods if it doesn't work with your natural rhythm. This is specifically how several people become tired out and finally surrender. You have recently taken the first big step. So, work at your own momentum. One other bad idea is to make hasty decisions to update the timeframes inappropriately. Start out slow and gradually put forth more effort toward your objective as the preparations progress. This ascertains you'll become totally primed to protect yourself in today's cyberwar.

While these strategies described here aren't foolproof, they are the best starting points for newcomers trying to protect yourself in today's cyberwar. There are definitely a lot of suggestions that you can accept to fit your preparation period, since you know your characteristic nature. Utilize this know-how, coupled with the plan revealed here to jump out there and finally protect yourself in today's cyberwar! If you are smart with how you invest your time, and fully apply all of the details here to calculate a workable plan, then you'll be a great guard in no time!

Do's and Don'ts of Protecting Yourself In Today's Cyberwar

Any hope of protecting yourself in today's cyberwar may be exhilarating coupled with scary. The well-known the National Rifle Association is a large progression in any guard's career. Initially that might sound impossible. However, with the appropriate briefing and foresight, protecting yourself in today's cyberwar can be conquered by everyone. Like any taxing challenge, protecting yourself in today's cyberwar may be conquered in a multitude of ways. Following are a couple thoughts which a guard ought to (and ought to not) think of:

Before Protecting Yourself In Today's Cyberwar

While the challenge is protecting yourself in today's cyberwar, there would be numerous concerns which a guard could do beforehand. This would assure that protecting yourself in today's cyberwar is not an overwhelming challenge.

DO Get A Copy Of Your Credit Report.

If you hope to protect yourself in today's cyberwar, you ought to be working for substantial time priming. This would physically help you to prevent identify theft and know your credit and bank account activity..

DON'T Forget To Shred Personal Information

It could be easy to neglect allowing your mind time off from preparing. However, this time of leisure prepares the mind to reflect on the aspiration of protecting yourself in today's cyberwar. Grant your mind time to reflect on meeting your ambitions so you avoid exhausting yourself.

DO Change Your Passwords And Make Them More Sophisticated After Every Nationwide Data Breach.

The introductory steps to protecting yourself in today's cyberwar is critical and by reflecting this painless guideline of changing your passwords and make them more sophisticated after every nationwide data breach., you would be carrying out whatever you should to prepare.

DON'T Give Your Social Security Number Out Like It's Halloween Candy

Say you skip over a milestones in the root of the preparations, that should not adversely impact the general objective provided you put forth the effort to get back on path. Avoid the inclination to intensifies the training inordinately, since doing so may push you to lose momentum.

While Protecting Yourself In Today's Cyberwar

DO Get Your Credit Report And Passwords Available If They Are Not In Your Brain.

Know what you can attain. Set your ambitions appropriately. By reflecting this guideline, you would feel confident and in control. and feel ready. Also, you would also relax the mind.

DON'T Get Involved With Phishing Scams On Your Computers, Pads And Phone

The most seasoned guard would be capable of protect yourself in today's cyberwar quicker. This is because they possibly have personal experience. Salvage your stamina and avoid comparing yourself with a different guard and compare your transition only with yourself.

DO Think Twice Before You Share Personal Information On Social Media Sites.

This is a critical guideline. By following this guideline in your career, you would feel confident and in control. coupled with feel ready. Additionally, you would relax the mind.

DON'T Give Passwords To Friends

There is no reason to analyze theories pertaining to protecting yourself in today's cyberwar. Following are specific instructions of whatever you should and should not try in order to succeed and finally secure yourself from today's cyberwar.

After Protecting Yourself In Today's Cyberwar

After priming to protect yourself in today's cyberwar,

remember, the progression is not complete! Following are a few do's, coupled with don'ts, to consider after you attain this goal:

DO Stay On Top Of Your Credit Report

DON'T Freak Out If You Get An Unauthorized Credit Inquiry On Your Credit Report

DO Observe And Evaluate Every Situation Involving Your Identification

DON'T Don't Leave Any Personal Credit Question Unanswered

These are a few relatively easy guidelines to incorporate while protecting yourself in today's cyberwar. Appreciate this progression and remember that the progression is yours!

How Protecting Yourself In Today's Cyberwar Will Change You

Protecting yourself in today's cyberwar is not for the weak-hearted. This could be incredibly difficult and the work does not become easier. However, if you would brave this work to the journey's end, you may find you aren't the same personality type that you had been before you started. Regardless of how well you train, something relating to just trying to protect yourself in today's cyberwar extends so many improvements.

To start with, you recognize how to protect yourself in today's cyberwar. Whether you prevail or fail, maintaining awareness of how to prepare is valuable to know. Despite the wealth of help and knowledge which you could find online or in traditional books, trying to protect yourself in today's cyberwar extends unique insights into how the many strategies work.

This sort of awareness not only results in maintaining awareness of your mind better, but more importantly gives you much required information for other endeavors.

Basically, protecting yourself in today's cyberwar proves how faithfully committed you are. Protecting yourself in today's cyberwar is a desire that lots of people have, but hardly a few have the focus and preparation to compete. Protecting yourself in today's cyberwar proves your dedication in the eyes of others, but more importantly it demonstrates it to your mind. The guts coupled with the willpower it entails to finish safeguarding personal information should not fall away after you accomplish your undertaking. Rather, they should remain a piece of you.

Protecting yourself in today's cyberwar helps your brain by showing you have whatever it requires to secure yourself from today's cyberwar. Protecting yourself in today's cyberwar also intensifies brainpower. When you protect yourself in today's cyberwar, you might be astounded by how you have made it to this point both intellectually and physically. You would be feeling those advantageous effects for several years.

Lastly, protecting yourself in today's cyberwar grants you bragging rights. So, not only can you share the exhilarating details of protecting yourself in today's cyberwar, with any of your friends, but you can share the phases of preparation. Furthermore, you recognize what you are capable of. Protecting yourself in today's cyberwar entails tons of courage, coupled with knowing you have whatever it requires to endeavor something so tough.

Protecting yourself in today's cyberwar definitely is difficult and challenging, but it changes you in several ways. It is no shocking surprise that only a few people succeed with protecting yourself in today's cyberwar. You would be showing yourself and the world that you have the strengths and awareness to endeavor some substantial things in life!

Protecting Yourself In Today's Cyberwar - The Lifestyle

It is instantly clear that people who aspire to protect yourself in today's cyberwar come in many shapes and sizes. However no matter the skill level, there are a few concerns which are common among those who hope to protect yourself in today's cyberwar. The reason tons of people who protect yourself in today's cyberwar have that vibe is because they have a lifestyle with corresponding values. That does not mean they live parallel lives, since that would be preposterous, and wrong. Those who protect yourself in today's cyberwar come from many walks of life. While they might not all have everything in common, there are a few lifestyle traits coupled with characteristics that they all possess.

Obviously this routine involves getting a copy of your credit report.. Without that, protecting yourself in today's cyberwar may become cumbersome. However, getting a copy of your credit report. is not strictly specific to just protecting yourself in today's cyberwar. Additionally, the routine involves changing your passwords and make them more sophisticated after every nationwide data breach. and following up on every security email alert from companies you are affiliated with.. Safeguarding personal information would need getting your credit report and passwords available if they are not in your brain. coupled with thinking twice before you share personal information on social media sites.. The fact is that safeguarding personal information is an investment. Additionally, monitoring credit and bank accounts cautiously. could lead to many sorts of unexpected benefits.

Because of that, many people who want to protect yourself in today's cyberwar, especially those who are strong-willed, would immediately see these additional advantages. These benefits do not develop entirely from getting your credit report and passwords available if they are not in your brain., either.

After investing so much effort in planning your everyday life to protect yourself in today's cyberwar, many people may find themselves naturally making better everyday choices in other areas of life. Those who have protect yourself in today's cyberwar possibly find that they would be ready to feel confident and in control. and feel ready. While that isn't a mystical skill that you would gain once you choose to protect yourself in today's cyberwar, that is one thing which would gradually include itself in your routine the deeper you prepare to safeguard personal information.

These benefits are substantial, but it can be really easy to be inundated without even seeing it. Say you have several friends who also would like to protect yourself in today's cyberwar, you might find that a few of them never concentrate on anything but protecting yourself in today's cyberwar. As with any life choice, some careful moderation is essential.

As you prepare for protecting yourself in today's cyberwar, you should find that these particular lifestyle adjustments are happening in your decisions. Getting your credit report and passwords available if they are not in your brain. coupled with thinking twice before you share personal information on social media sites. makes sense in lots of ways, and therefore, you will feel confident and in control. coupled with protect your information. The lifestyle is very difficult, but it is definitely worth it. Say you tough it out, protecting yourself in today's cyberwar and the associated routine would make your life better in many ways.

Is Protecting Yourself In Today's Cyberwar Right For You?

Those who choose to protect yourself in today's cyberwar are really strong-willed. There are lots of things in life which can't be faked. You can't fake a job interview, or the outcome of finals in school. Equally, you can't fake protecting yourself in today's cyberwar. You simply can't protect yourself in today's cyberwar without some foresight. Safeguarding personal information entails one to be protective and strong-willed. It entails 5 days of training vigilantly.

When you are planning your routine to protect yourself in today's cyberwar, be sure that you do not forget to shred personal information. Also, do not attempt to give your social security number out like it's halloween candy. Preparation entails time and it cannot be rushed. By darting through the preparation period, you will not truly be training and it can be concluded that you faked your efforts through the steps. Doing it the appropriate way will allow you to have longevity toward your results.

Protecting yourself in today's cyberwar could be quite exhilarating and gives a feeling of accomplishment that you would value for ever. Protecting yourself in today's cyberwar is a challenge. Whether you would be new or are totally seasoned, there are rational pros and cons with protecting yourself in today's cyberwar.

There are additional advantages with protecting yourself in today's cyberwar and the biggest one is that it would offer you a feeling of pride and accomplishment. Safeguarding personal information is a tough activity. Protecting yourself in today's cyberwar is an action that might typically remind you of your dedication and offer you a feeling of fulfillmement for merely trying this activity.

A different great benefit of protecting yourself in today's cyberwar is that it refines your scheduling skills since you would have to plan how you would move forward to really secure yourself from today's cyberwar. So after you choose to protect yourself in today's cyberwar, you might learn a great deal about planning coupled with staying focused.

There are indisputable benefits to protecting yourself in today's cyberwar. It is not as simple as it looks. There could be a few limitations that you might have to get around, like the investment of time essential to prepare. You need to offer yourself 5 days, and make a full commitment. Do not try to prepare in bits and pieces. Devotion coupled with sincere effort ought to finally allow you to secure yourself from today's cyberwar.

This may offer you a little insight to establish if protecting yourself in today's cyberwar is suitable for you. Without a doubt, protecting yourself in today's cyberwar definitely needs one to become protective, defensive and securing. When you see yourself as the personality type with these particular attributes, you might be completely able to secure yourself from today's cyberwar.

The most critical thing to be aware of is there are definitely no shortcuts. Many people who have recently protect yourself in today's cyberwar perceive how much dedication is essential. You need to hear your inner voice, which will bring you through the steps to protecting yourself in today's cyberwar.

Benefits of Protecting Yourself In Today's Cyberwar

Whenever you safeguard personal information, there are typically some critical steps that you need to achieve. You would have to get your credit report and passwords available if they are not in your brain., think twice before you share personal information on social media sites., and monitor credit and bank accounts cautiously.. These three steps do not just help anyone out with protecting yourself in today's cyberwar, they more importantly bring other improvements to life. Safeguarding personal information is an action which has made countless men and women everywhere feel better about themselves.

Those who were getting your credit report and passwords

available if they are not in your brain. possibly see slight adjustments with their mental well-being. These people more importantly feel primed to tackle more in life. Priming in advance allows you to be stronger compared to what you had been before. This allows you to take on more than you possibly had before, and not lose stamina as easily. It all benefits you, and that more importantly assists you in your natural decisions.

You have recently categorized yourself as a protective and defensive personality type. Every securing self-starter is usually tailored to protect yourself in today's cyberwar.

Many people think twice before you share personal information on social media sites. while they prepare to protect yourself in today's cyberwar. Apparently, thinking twice before you share personal information on social media sites. has many benefits aside from merely protecting your information and controlling your identity. You may also find that you can relieve stress. All this would make you feel better on a daily basis.

Safeguarding personal information definitely results in preventing identify theft. It results from monitoring credit and bank accounts cautiously., especially when done over a longer term of time. Additionally, that brings tons of additional benefits. To start with, you can know your credit and bank account activity.. Additionally you would monitor your credit score.

Protecting yourself in today's cyberwar is an activity where everyone can typically improve themselves through the preparation period. While training could be up to 5 days, that means that you may presumably have to prepare typically for a term of time. Protecting yourself in today's cyberwar would make you be stronger and better primed for your everyday challenges.

After Protecting Yourself In Today's Cyberwar - What To Do

Protecting yourself in today's cyberwar is no easy task, and many times individuals do not consider the things they would like to do after they secure yourself from today's cyberwar. So much time is spent on preparing, yet hardly a thought is given to the recovery strategy. While focusing on safeguarding personal information is critical, you should also consider the things you would like to experience afterwards. There is no doubt you will feel better about yourself upon achieving your aspiration to secure yourself from today's cyberwar.

Be sure to facilitate time to redeem yourself from protecting yourself in today's cyberwar. Say you are new at protecting yourself in today's cyberwar, then it is best to proceed slow. To decrease the time it may take to get back on path, here are some ways to help your mind recover.

After protecting yourself in today's cyberwar, be sure to stay on top of your credit report. You need to also be sure to observe and evaluate every situation involving your identification. It will physically help you recoup all of the stamina that you expended on protecting yourself in today's cyberwar. Also, be really careful not to freak out if you get an unauthorized credit inquiry on your credit report. That would impede your general recovery. Additionally, be sure you do not don't leave any personal credit question unanswered.

After protecting yourself in today's cyberwar, you might become burned out physically and intellectually. After working for 5 days training for your goal, it is common to want a little time to rest. During the time you are in your moment of relaxation, it is a sensible idea to reflect on the things you might want to achieve next. While you do not need another specific goal in mind, it is a sensible idea to develop a rough idea where you wish to go next. Though remember, do not get into something new right away. Make sure you are completely recovered so you may ensure that you are genuinely ready. You can potentially cause harm to yourself by pushing too hard. This is the reason that moment of leisure is so critical.

This is an advantage of permitting yourself to rest. Then develop your plan. It could be difficult to keep training without a specific goal in mind. When you produce a solid plan, you could start right away.

You would not need to get right back to training after you attain your aspiration. Take a few weeks to recover. Just remember not to strain your spirit so you have the momentum to accomplish your other objectives!

Common Questions About Protecting Yourself In Today's Cyberwar

By now, you may be informed of the preparations you ought to take to protect yourself in today's cyberwar. Say you identify a question which hasn't been covered, do not agonize. Following are a few common questions which surface with protecting yourself in today's cyberwar:

Is it feasible to protect yourself in today's cyberwar for free?

For most people, it is feasible to protect yourself in today's cyberwar for free. It is unnecessary to put forth tons of money preparing to protect yourself in today's cyberwar. Following are a couple suggestions to manage costs.

- Start with a free copy of your credit report each year. You can get a free copy at www.annualcreditreport.com. You may want to look into their identity protection program or look into their real-time alerts.

- Attempt to keep all your personal information private.

Go the extra mile and give unsolicited callers zero information. Sometimes it's best to hang up the phone before they can even verify your name.

- No more 1, 2, 3, A, B, C, passwords! Using names and birth dates can be cracked easy. Create passwords that only you know and put them in your lock box.

One other question which frequently comes up while anyone is planning to protect yourself in today's cyberwar is regarding the common "rules" to consider while safeguarding personal information. Below are a few practices to be mindful of:

- While getting your credit report and passwords available if they are not in your brain., Remember to know exactly where your passwords and and credit report are. This will equipped to take on the cyber attack immediately.

- Typically, thinking twice before you share personal information on social media sites. is critical when safeguarding personal information. This will dispatching unsolicited information should be stopped so you will not get unsolicited viruses in return.

- As you narrow in on monitoring credit and bank accounts cautiously., be sure to Report any and all unusual activity. This will update all activity.

You have successfully taken the first step toward protecting yourself in today's cyberwar by reading about it. Undoubtedly additional questions may surface and another way you may benefit yourself is by approaching this objective with a friend who may have similar objectives.

Oftentimes a "buddy system" is a great solution when approaching a desire which requires a protective and defensive personality. While you may ultimately protect yourself in today's cyberwar by yourself, it makes sense to connect with someone upon a parallel progression to go over obstacles as they arise. Be conscious to select like-minded companions and steer clear from people who are uncertain or careless, since they might steer you away approaching your objectives.

Remember all the questions you responded to just a bit ago?

Do you have valuable information and assets that you want to protect?

Do you think your the best person to protect your information?

Can you afford to lose your identify and life savings?

You would have answered "yes" to the questions which determined you have the ideal attitude to succeed at protecting yourself in today's cyberwar. Choose a friend who may also answer "yes" to these particular questions since they may also be inclined to succeed at protecting yourself in today's cyberwar.

Best of wishes on protecting yourself in today's cyberwar!

www.ingramcontent.com/pod-product-compliance
Lightning Source LLC
Chambersburg PA
CBHW051217050326
40689CB00008B/1345